Collins

Easy Learning

Writing practice

Age 7-9

My name is _____.

I am _____ years old.

I go to _____ School.

How to use this book

- Find a quiet, comfortable place to work, away from other distractions.
- Tackle one topic at a time.
- It is important your child reads the information and questions carefully.
- Help with reading the information and instructions where necessary and ensure your child understands what to do.
- Encourage your child to check their own answers as they complete each activity.
- Discuss your child's answers with them.
- Let your child return to their favourite pages once they have been completed.
- Reward your child with plenty of praise and encouragement.

Special features

- Yellow boxes: Introduce a topic and outline the key writing ideas.
- Red boxes: Emphasise a rule relating to the unit.
- Yellow shaded boxes: Offer advice to parents on how to consolidate your child's understanding.

Published by Collins
An imprint of HarperCollins*Publishers*
77–85 Fulham Palace Road
Hammersmith
London
W6 8JB

Browse the complete Collins catalogue at
www.collinseducation.com

First published in 2012

© HarperCollins*Publishers* 2012

10 9 8 7 6 5 4 3 2 1

ISBN-13 978-0-00-746727-3

British Library Cataloguing in Publication Data

A Catalogue record for this publication is available from the British Library

Page design and layout by G Brasnett, Cambridge
Illustrated by Steve Evans, Rachel Annie Bridgen, Kathy Baxendale and Andy Tudor
Cover design by Linda Miles, Lodestone Publishing
Cover illustration by Kathy Baxendale
Commissioned by Tammy Poggo
Project managed by Katie Galloway
Printed in China

Contents

Story openings

It is always important to make the **opening** of your story *interesting*.

An interesting opening invites the reader to discover more about your story.

Read these story openings and answer the questions.

Opening 1

The waves tickled my feet as I walked along the beach. It was early in the morning and no one else was awake. The peace and quiet gave me time to think. How were we going to get off this island and continue our journey home?

Opening 2

I sleepily crawled out of bed and opened my curtains. The sun was out and the birds were singing. I could hear mum downstairs busy in the kitchen. Suddenly I remembered. Today I was starting at my new school. I wanted to crawl back into bed and hide.

Q1 What time of day are these openings set?

_____

Q2 Which opening tells you what the weather is like?

_____

Q3 Which story would you like to read more of? Why?

_____

_____

_____

Sit down with your child and look at story openings found in books you have at home.
Discuss the openings and talk about those that you both find interesting.

4

Settings

A **setting** helps a reader to imagine where the story is taking place.

It is like painting a picture but using words instead of paints.

Look at these pictures.

Q1 Describe these settings as clearly as you can using interesting words.

Setting 1

_____

_____

_____

_____

_____

Setting 2

_____

_____

_____

_____

_____

Discuss the settings your child has written. Highlight some good descriptive words that your child has used. How might the writing be improved further?

Characters

Your writing will always be more interesting when the **characters** you are writing about are described clearly.

Look at this character.

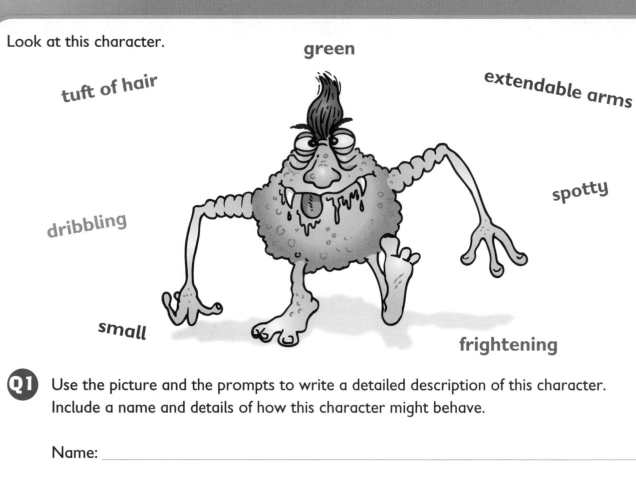

green

tuft of hair

extendable arms

spotty

dribbling

small

frightening

Q1 Use the picture and the prompts to write a detailed description of this character. Include a name and details of how this character might behave.

Name: _____

_____

_____

_____

_____

_____

_____

_____

Q2 Now write a character profile of someone you know.

Try to include as much detail as you can – not just what the person looks like but also write about their personality and their likes and dislikes.

Include either a photo or a drawing of the person you are describing and write their name.

_____

_____

_____

_____

_____

_____

_____

_____

Writing a story

When you write a story you need to think about:
- Your story **opening**.
- Who the main **characters** are.
- What happens at the **beginning**, **middle** and **end**.

Choose one of these story openings.

Opening 1

The waves tickled my feet as I walked along the beach. It was early in the morning and no one else was awake. The peace and quiet gave me time to think. How were we going to get off this island and continue our journey home?

Opening 2

I sleepily crawled out of bed and opened my curtains. The sun was out and the birds were singing. I could hear mum downstairs busy in the kitchen. Suddenly I remembered. Today I was starting at my new school. I wanted to crawl back into bed and hide.

You are going to continue the story, but before you do you need to plan it.
Think about whether the character you wrote about on page 7 would fit into this story.

Q1 Make notes in the following boxes.

Beginning

Middle

End

Q2 Continue the story here. Give it a title.

_____

_____

_____

_____

_____

_____

_____

_____

_____

_____

_____

_____

_____

_____

_____

_____

_____

_____

Q2 Discuss your child's story plan before they start writing the story. This will help your child to consolidate their ideas. Extra paper may be needed.

Writing a playscript

A story can be turned into a **playscript**.

> The playscript needs to begin by **setting the scene**.
> The **conversations** need to be set out clearly without speech marks.
> **Stage directions** need to be clear so the actors know what to do.

Look carefully at how the beginning of this story has been turned into a playscript.

Story

"Please can Katie come home for tea?" asked Dan.

"No, I'm afraid we have to go out tonight," his mum answered as they walked home from school.

"But why? I didn't know we were going out!" Dan said.

"I think you will be very pleased once you know where we are going," replied Mum.

"Really? Tell me now!" Dan excitedly jumped up and down.

"I want to surprise you but not long to wait, just until Dad gets home," said Mum as she opened the front door.

Playscript

Dan has just met his mum at the end of the school day.
They are walking home from school.

Dan   Please can Katie come home for tea?

Mum   No, I'm afraid we have to go out tonight.

Dan   But why? I didn't know we were going out!

Mum   I think you will be very pleased once you know where we are going.

Dan   *(jumping up and down excitedly)*
          Really? Tell me now!

Mum opens the front door.

Mum   I want to surprise you but not long to wait, just until Dad gets home.

Q1 What do you think happens next in the story?
Plan what you think might happen next.
Where do you think Mum is going to take Dan?

Notes

Q2 Continue the story but write it as a playscript.

Remember to:
- Include changes in scenes or places.
- Include stage directions.
- Lay out speech correctly.

Looking at poems

Poems can use rhyming words but they don't have to.

Read this poem.

This is a fun poem that describes a favourite food.
Some of the lines in each verse rhyme, but not all of them.

Spaghetti! Spaghetti!

Spaghetti! spaghetti!
you're wonderful stuff,
I love you, spaghetti,
I can't get enough.
You're covered in sauce
and you're sprinkled with cheese,
spaghetti! spaghetti!
oh, give me some more please.

Spaghetti! spaghetti!
piled high in a mound,
you wiggle, you wiggle,
you squiggle around.
There's slurpy spaghetti
all over my plate,
spaghetti! spaghetti!
I think you are great.

Spaghetti! spaghetti!
I love you a lot,
you're slishy, you're sloshy,
delicious and hot.
I gobble you down
oh, I can't get enough,
spaghetti! spaghetti!
you're wonderful stuff.

Jack Prelutsky

Look at the first verse of *Spaghetti! Spaghetti!* again.

 Underline the rhyming words.

> Spaghetti! spaghetti!
> you're wonderful stuff,
> I love you, spaghetti,
> I can't get enough.
> You're covered in sauce
> and you're sprinkled with cheese,
> spaghetti! spaghetti!
> oh, give me some more please.

 Now write your own verse about your favourite food.

Notice how each line in *Spaghetti! Spaghetti!* has a rhythm or beat – as in music. Your poem could have a similar rhythm.

Different types of poem

Some poems have a special structure, making them a particular type of poem.

This topic looks at some different examples.

Haiku poems

This poem is called a **Haiku**.
Haikus were first written in Japan.

Read this poem.

> Haiku poems don't rhyme.
> A Haiku always has a total of 17 syllables: 5 syllables in the first line, 7 in the second line and 5 in the last line.

Winter Frost

Sparkling shimmer
Birds hunt glistening berries
Bare trees look chilly

Q1 Write your own Haiku.
Remember to have the correct number of syllables in each line.
Write a Haiku about **summer**.

_____

_____

_____

_____

Look for other examples of Haiku poems with your child. (Many can be found on the internet.)
Ask your child to check the number of syllables in each poem.

Acrostic poems

The poems on this page are called **acrostic** poems.

Barney

Brave
Arty
Runner
Naughty
Excitable
Young

> The first letter of each line spells a word.
>
> An acrostic poem can have one word or more than one word on each line.
>
> It doesn't have to rhyme.

Martian

Made a landing on our street
Arrived in a pink spaceship
Ran out the door and then stood
Taking in the concrete houses and metal cars
In an instant he had returned to his ship
Aghast at what he saw
Never to return again!

Q2 Write your own acrostic poem about a holiday.

Holiday

H_____

O_____

L_____

I_____

D_____

A_____

Y_____

Note taking

Look at this extract about Barack Obama, the first African-American to be elected as an American president.

Barack Obama

Barack Obama was born on the 4th August 1961, in Hawaii. Obama's mother grew up in the USA and his father was born in Kenya. They met at the University of Hawaii and married on 2nd February, 1961.

Obama's parents divorced when he was only two years old. In 1966, Barack's mother married again and the family moved to Indonesia. At the age of ten, Barack was sent back to Hawaii to live with his grandparents. While living with his grandparents, Obama went to the highly thought of Punahou Academy, where he did really well in basketball.

Obama was unhappy because he missed his father. His father wrote to him often but he only visited Obama once. When Obama was 22 years old he received the news that his father had died in a car accident in Kenya. Although he missed his father he became very close to his grandparents.

Below are notes made from the first paragraph. The underlined words highlight the important information in the paragraph. This information can then be written as notes.

Barack Obama was born on the <u>4th August 1961</u>, in <u>Hawaii</u>. Obama's <u>mother</u> grew up in the <u>USA</u> and his <u>father</u> was born in <u>Kenya</u>. They met at the <u>University</u> of Hawaii and <u>married</u> on <u>2nd February, 1961</u>.

Notes on first paragraph
Obama born 4th August 1961
Born in Hawaii
Mother from USA
Father from Kenya
Parents met at University, married Feb 1961

Q1 Complete these notes about the second paragraph. Again, the key information has been underlined.

> Obama's <u>parents divorced</u> when he was only <u>two years old</u>. In <u>1966</u>, Barack's mother married again and the family <u>moved to Indonesia</u>. At the age of <u>ten</u>, Barack was sent <u>back to Hawaii</u> to live with his <u>grandparents</u>. While living with his grandparents, Obama went to the highly thought of <u>Punahou Academy</u>, where he did really well in <u>basketball</u>.

Obama's parents divorced when he was _____ .

Mum remarried.

Family moved to _____ .

Aged 10 Obama moved back to _____

Lived with _____

Went to _____

Good at _____ .

Q2 Look at the final paragraph.
Underline the key information then write your own notes for it.

> Obama was unhappy because he missed his father. His father wrote to him often but he only visited Obama once. When Obama was 22 years old he received the news that his father had died in a car accident in Kenya. Although he missed his father he became very close to his grandparents.

Editing is a way of *improving what you have written.*

When you read through what you have written:
- Check that your punctuation is correct.
- Check that you don't repeat yourself.
- Make sure you use interesting words.
- Use pronouns and don't repeat nouns.
- Join short sentences with connectives.

Look carefully at this short extract.

The words highlighted in red show where improvements can be made, either by removing words or by adding new ones.

> Keita, the bouncy puppy, raced up the muddy lane.
> Keita didn't look back. Her owner called her. Keita
> loved the exercise and loved the mud!
>
> Eventually she was caught by her owner and told off.
> Keita was tired and thirsty. All the effort had been
> worth it. She had loved her moment of freedom.

> *Keita, the bouncy puppy, raced up the muddy lane. She*
> *didn't look back as her owner called her. Keita loved the*
> *exercise and the mud!*
>
> *Eventually she was caught and told off. Keita was*
> *exhausted and thirsty. All the effort had been worth it*
> *because she had loved her moment of freedom.*

It is important for your child to learn that what they write can be improved, but they need guidance to see where to make these improvements. Look at a piece of your child's written work and discuss with them where improvements can be made.

Q1 Read through this extract and then edit it.
Begin by underlining words or phrases you think can be improved.
Write notes around the extract with your ideas.

Remember to:
- Watch out for words that are repeated.
- Add interesting words.
- Add pronouns instead of repeating nouns.
- Join short sentences with connectives.

> Keita's owner was not very pleased. He knew he had to clean
>
> Keita before putting Keita in the car. To the owner's delight he
>
> spotted a stream. It ran down the side of a field. At first Keita
>
> bounced in an excited way towards the stream. As they got
>
> close Keita looked more nervous. It was noisy, cold and strange.
>
> Maybe her moment of freedom hadn't been worth it after all!

Once you feel you have made all the changes you need, write the paragraph out neatly.

_____

_____

_____

_____

_____

_____

_____

Newspaper reports

A **newspaper report** has:
- a *headline* that draws the reader to the report;
- an *opening paragraph* which tells the reader the most important details and sets the scene;
- *further paragraphs* which have interesting information about the subject.

Read this newspaper report.

Cheeky chimps on the motorway

Drivers were surprised to see monkeys running all over the road yesterday.

The lorry taking them to their new home at Burwell Zoo had broken down. While the driver went to get help, one of the monkeys managed to lift the latch on the door.

Inspector Baker said the monkeys looked like they were having great fun.

They climbed all over the road signs and scrambled up the lamp posts. One even sat on top of the police car!

Some drivers got irate because of the traffic jam, but most drivers were prepared to see the funny side.

"I'm pleased to say all the cheeky chimps are now safely back in the zoo," said Inspector Baker last night.

Look at newspaper reports with your child.
Discuss their structure and the different types of subjects that are covered.

Q1 Write your own newspaper report. Your report needs to be less than 60 words. These notes give you the information you need for your report.

What happened
Motorbike rider had fun in school field and ruined football pitch.
Motorbike rider not caught – ask for witnesses?

Where
South Masey Primary School

When
21st October, during the night

Key witnesses
School caretaker (Mrs Kembrey) – woken at 1.30am then called police
PC Walsh – arrived at scene just after motorbike rider had left

Damage
Football pitch pitted with skid marks. Many white lines disturbed.
Goal netting damaged

Reaction
Headteacher (Mr Morris) – devastated, no money to sort damage
Children – very upset. Want to raise money to help.

Letter writing

Letters are written for many reasons but they all need to be set out in a similar way.

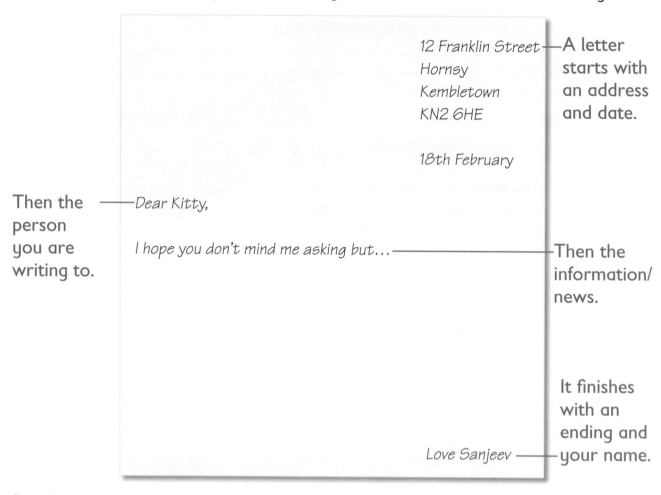

12 Franklin Street — A letter starts with an address and date.
Hornsy
Kembletown
KN2 6HE

18th February

Then the person you are writing to. — Dear Kitty,

I hope you don't mind me asking but… — Then the information/news.

It finishes with an ending and your name.

Love Sanjeev — your name.

Some letters are written to **complain** about something.
Complaint letters are set out the same way but the information in the letter has to be very clear, *stating the problem*, *giving details* and then finishing with *a conclusion*.

Q1 Write a letter from your home address to Mr Hanwell at the local council. Mr Hanwell has decided to shut the local playground because he says the equipment is too old and unsafe for children to play on.

● First, write notes on what you think of Mr Hanwell's plans. Do you think it is a good idea? Why? What could be done about the unsafe equipment?

Notes

● Now write your letter.

_____,

Explanations

A written **explanation** provides information about something.

Look carefully at this diagram. It shows the water cycle.
This is the process of what happens to the water on our Earth.

Water cycle

Rain falls on the hills and seeps into the soil.

Moisture cools and makes cloud droplets.

Water seeps through the soil and into streams and rivers.

Water turns to moisture and rises.

Small streams and rivers flow into bigger rivers and eventually into the sea.

The oceans store huge quantities of water.

Q1 Use the information you find in the diagram to write an explanation of what happens.

The Water Cycle

To start with, the water _____

_____

_____

It then _____

_____

_____

After this _____

_____

_____

As a result _____

_____

_____

Then _____

_____

_____

Finally _____

_____

Description

Adding **description** to your writing makes it more interesting.

the **silent**, **slithering** snake

These notes have been made about an animal park based in a city centre.

'Amazing Animals' in Bristol City Centre

Open 9 a.m. – 5 p.m. daily
Free parking

Animals to feed: goats
                   sheep
                   chickens
                   ducks
Animals to ride: ponies
Animals to hold: chicks
                   rabbits
                   guinea pigs

– Unlimited fun all year round with a playground and sand area
– Live entertainment in the summer
– Opportunities to handle and look after the animals
– Milk a goat!

Family ticket - half price in January and February

Q1 Use the information to write a recount of a visit you made to the park.

Include in your recount three things you found interesting or entertaining, for example, feeding an animal, eating lunch, falling off a swing, getting lost.

Add description to make your writing more interesting. Describe how you felt, how things tasted, how they looked and how they sounded and smelt.

Notes

Look at the recount your child has written. Discuss how many adjectives your child has used. Could more description have been used? Discuss this with your child.

Instructions give us directions and an order in which to do things.

Instructions should have:
- a list of everything needed;
- clear step-by-step directions;
- sometimes a picture to help.

> Instructions must be clear and easy to follow.

Read these instructions about how to play 'Stuck in the Mud', a playground game.

Stuck in the Mud

You need: 4 or more children (the more the better)

1 Decide who is going to be the catcher.
2 The rest of the group runs around.
3 When the catcher tags someone they have to stand still (as if stuck in the mud) with their arms out.
4 Another member of the group can free the stuck person by crawling through their legs.
5 The game is over when the catcher has made everyone stuck in the mud!

Look at other types of instructions with your child, for example, how to make or cook something, how to get from one place to the next, how to clean out a pet's cage.

Q1 Now write your own instructions.

Choose a game you enjoy playing and write instructions for it.
It might be a board game, a card game, a playground game or a made-up
game you play.

You need:

Instructions:

Picture:

Writing a poem

Poems can be written about anything and anyone.
They are a way of expressing your thoughts.

This poem was written by Robert Louis Stevenson over 150 years ago.

The Cow

The friendly cow, all red and white,
I love with all my heart:
She gives me cream with all her might,
To eat with apple-tart.

She wanders lowing here and there,
And yet she cannot stray,
All in the pleasant open air,
The pleasant light of day;

And blown by all the winds that pass
And wet with all the showers,
She walks among the meadow grass
And eats the meadow flowers.

Robert Louis Stevenson obviously loves the cow.
His poem shows how closely he has watched the cow.
His poem is a clear picture of what the cow's life is like.

Choose any subject you find very interesting.
Here are some ideas:

Places

Family

Famous people

Hobbies

Food

Sport

Pets

Friends

Q1 Write your own poem on something you find interesting.

Write a poem that has **two verses**.

You need to decide if your poem is going to rhyme.

Start by noting words and phrases you might use.

Notes

_____

_____

_____

_____

_____

_____

_____

_____

_____

_____

Answers

Story openings

Page 4

1 Both story openings are set at the beginning of the day.

2 Opening 2 tells you what the weather is like.

3 Child's own answer, giving reasons why.

Settings

Page 5

1 Child's own descriptions of the two settings.

Characters

Pages 6–7

1 Child's description of the alien character pictured, including words given as prompts: green, spotty, dribbling, tuft of hair, extendable arms, frightening and small.

2 Character description of someone your child knows.

Writing a story

Pages 8–9

1 Evidence of planning is important.

2 Child's own story using one of the openings given.

Writing a playscript

Pages 10–11

1 Child's own notes.

2 Child's playscript of the continuing story.

It is important it is laid out as the example on page 10.

Looking at poems

Pages 12–13

1 Spaghetti! spaghetti!
you're wonderful <u>stuff</u>,
I love you, spaghetti,
I can't get <u>enough</u>.
You're covered in sauce
and you're sprinkled with <u>cheese</u>,
Spaghetti! spaghetti!
oh, give me some more <u>please</u>.

2 Child's poem describing their favourite food.

Different types of poem

Pages 14–15

1 Child's Haiku about summer.
(Must follow rules given on page 14.)

2 Child's acrostic poem about a holiday.
(Must follow rules given on page 15.)

Note-taking

Pages 16–17

1 Obama's parents divorced when he was **2 years old**.
Mum remarried.
Family moved to **Indonesia**.
Aged 10 Obama moved back to **Hawaii**.
Lived with **grandparents**.
Went to **Punahou Academy**.
Good at **basketball**.

2 Child's own notes on final paragraph.

Editing

Pages 18–19

1 E.g. Keita's owner was not very pleased as he knew he had to clean Keita before putting her in the car. To the owner's delight he spotted a stream that ran down the side of a field. At first Keita bounced excitably towards the stream but as they got close she looked more nervous. It was noisy, cold and strange. Maybe her moment of freedom hadn't been worth it after all!